Contents

SECTION 2:

Manchester City Council Education Department

C ... *ion*

l

A Cros ...
inv ...
inte ...
'Speaker & Listener'

Sue Skelton

Manchester University School of Education

1990

David Fulton Publishers Ltd
2 Barbon Close, London WC1N 3JX

First published in Great Britain by
David Fulton Publishers, 1990
Reprinted 1992

British Library of Cataloguing in Publication Data
Aherne, Pam
   Communication for all
   1. Man. Communication. Role of language
   I. Title   II. Thornber, Ann
   400

   ISBN 1-85346-168-7 ✓

Typeset by Manchester University School of Education
Printed in Great Britain by Bell and Bain Ltd., Glasgow

Acknowledgements

Sincere thanks go to our colleagues, who at short notice have given up their valuable time to read the draft versions of this document. In particular we thank Peter Mittler, Juliet Goldbart and the language coordinators and staff of the six Manchester schools for pupils with severe and complex learning difficulties.

Our warmest thanks go to the pupils we teach and their parents, who have made us realise and appreciate that communication encompasses far more than just speech and language.

Finally, we acknowledge Vic Johnson whose skill, dedication and patience in computer technology have made this document possible.

Introduction

The introduction of the National Curriculum has posed many questions as to whether English: Speaking and Listening should have a 'pre' or 'foundation' level to give ease of entry for some pupils with learning difficulties.

Having an *alternative* in the form of a 'pre' or 'foundation' level will automatically exclude some pupils from what the Education Reform Act (1988) claims as being a curriculum for ALL. This document is part of the work being developed by Manchester Teacher Fellows illustrating that the education offered to ALL pupils irrespective of need, can and indeed should include the National Curriculum. Every pupil is therefore seen to be working within level 1 or above (see Entitlement for All In Practice 1990, Fagg, Aherne, Skelton and Thornber; Science for All, 1990, Fagg, Skelton, Aherne and Thornber; Mathematics for All, 1990, Aherne, Thornber, Fagg and Skelton).

This document examines attainment target 1 (AT1): Speaking and Listening, in the English National Curriculum (1989). It aims to assist colleagues in making the attainment targets and programmes of study at Key Stage 1 more fully accessible for pupils with special needs. In particular, this work is concerned with those learners who have severe and complex difficulties and who may use non verbal means of communication more effectively than speech.

A footnote to the statutory AT acknowledges that *'pupils unable to communicate by speech may use other means'.* Other areas of the National Curriculum documentation place strong emphasis on communication; attainment target 1 of science, attainment targets 1 and 9 of mathematics, attainment target 4 of technology. Significant documentation relating to communication is incorporated into Curriculum Guidance 3 The Whole Curriculum (NCC 1990).

Communication (oracy, literacy) is described as a cross-curricular skill which is:

> *'transferable, chiefly independent of content and can be developed in different contexts across the whole curriculum.'*

> *'The National Curriculum considers it absolutely essential that these skills are fostered across the whole curriculum in a measured and planned way.'*

In order to incorporate the needs of all pupils, this document sets Speaking and Listening into the wider context of the **process** of **communication.** Effective interpersonal communication includes the use of tone, gestures, signs and body language to fully express meanings or feelings and to demonstrate listening. Learning to understand and use these social aspects is important for all pupils and for those who have limited or no use of speech, they are vital.

Section 1 discusses current understanding of how children, from their earliest interactions with others, develop language and non verbal forms of communication. A process is identified in which learning depends on the quality of interactions between 'speaker and listener'. This process ensures that children **want** to communicate, that there is **someone** to communicate with and **something** to communicate about. It also requires teaching pupils that communication is enjoyable and brings results. Elements of the communicative process such as speaking, using non vocal alternatives, and listening are seen as being interrelated rather than as distinct learning areas. Implications arise for extended programmes of study and targets for attainment within Level 1.

Section 2 presents a working model of the process of communication so that the elements and skills involved are clarified for practice. Areas of need for learners with difficulties may thus be more easily identified. AT1 in English is represented in this format, which combines statements of attainment, examples and programmes of study. Skills to be taught and corresponding programmes of study to be followed at various stages of development and experience within Level 1 are then presented in an interactive framework. Further resources are suggested at each stage which may guide assessment and intervention strategies needed to meet a wide range of individual needs.

The Appendix gives two examples of topic webs featuring communication as a cross-curricular skill.

SECTION 1:
Foundations of
Communication

Over the past twenty years there have been exciting developments in our understanding of how children communicate and our approach to teaching spoken language is changing. The reasons for this may be summarised as follows.

• There has been a growing understanding of how children learn. Learning occurs through all of the interactions between the child and his/her social and physical environment. For the child, areas of learning are interrelated rather than compartmentalised into subject headings.

• The traditional emphasis on language development as a growing collection of words and grammatical forms, has changed. We are now much more concerned with **how** children use language and what they are communicating **about**.

• The evidence of research into the way children learn to communicate has given rise to new approaches. In short, children learn to communicate by participating in the communication process with others. To do so, they need a reason to communicate, someone to communicate with and a means of expressing themselves. Learning depends on the quality of the interactions in which they are involved.

All these issues are well documented and are as relevant for students with severe and profound learning difficulties as for other learners. In this introductory section, some of the implications for practice in the context of the National Curriculum are considered.

(Adapted from Aherne 1990.)

The Function and Nature of Communication

Halliday (1973) suggested that children know what language **is** because they know what language **does** and that it is essential to discover:

> *'the purposes language serves for us ... how we achieve*
>
> *these purposes through speaking and listening, reading*
>
> *and writing.....and how language itself has been shaped by*
>
> *use.'*

He stresses childrens' use of language to express their understanding of the world and its meaning for them, as well as expressing needs, feelings etc. The context for this is grounded in the child's own direct experience, and the function of language is fundamentally a social need to communicate. Thus both the intellectual and the social bases of communication are identified. Intellectual understanding influences the content and meaning and social relationships influence its use and effectiveness. Two new theoretical approaches which have arisen from numerous studies are known as the psycholinguistic and the sociolinguistic approach. (See Goldbart 1988a for a more detailed account.)

As evolving theories show, the linguistic, intellectual and social aspects of the situation in which children acquire language are dependent upon each other, and evolve in a mutually supportive way. **Hence the skills or attainment targets to be identified in the development of the process of communication, including speaking and listening, should have three main components: intellectual, linguistic and social.**

Kiernan, Reid and Goldbart (1987) define communication as:

> *'responses which a person makes intentionally in order to*
>
> *affect the behaviour of another person and with the*

expectation that the other person will receive and act on that message.'

These responses include speaking, listening and using language as a system of words and rules. However they also include the use of non verbal elements of communication such as gesture, expression and body language. The latter reflect social or 'pragmatic' aspects such as the act a speaker intends to carry out with a sentence or word, for example commanding, questioning. The speaker presupposes that the listener shares their understanding between what is communicated and the situation. For example, a glance at a friend in a group situation can mean any thing from 'its time to go' or 'don't say any more about that'.

Current studies focus upon the social 'rules' and use of communication. The importance of these pragmatic aspects of communication with their roots in social interaction has been highlighted by McLean and Snyder-McLean (1985). This perspective has been expanded upon and developed for all children including those with severe learning difficulties.

The use of tone, facial expression and body language may convey as much or more than spoken words. We can, and indeed all do, communicate non-verbally both in socially understood ways and in ways which are more personal and most fully understood by family and friends.

Early Development Within Level 1 of The National Curriculum

Most published language schemes do little to meet the needs of learners who are not ready to use words for communication. This is partly because the intellectual stage of understanding necessary to participate in them may not yet have been reached.

Recent approaches offer an understanding of the development of communication from an early stage, which enable us to more effectively meet the needs of learners. The content of communication, including spoken language, is concerned with the meanings an individual tries to convey and reflect his/her stage of understanding of the world, as do the strategies s/he uses to express these meanings. Thus it is important to enable all learners to develop a range of ways of acting upon their environment and to progress through stages of intellectual understanding first identified by Piaget (1953). Further assessment procedures for these stages have been developed by Uzgiris and Hunt (1975) and Coupe and Levy (1985). The latter is specifically related to children and young people who have severe and profound learning difficulties.

Facilitating perceptual development is necessary for the development of communication but it is not enough without the development of the functional use of communication in the social context. Such development is summarised and outlined in its early stages by Goldbart (1988a) as Figure 1 overleaf illustrates. Some functions of communication are summarised by Kiernan and Reid (1987), and for those learners who have not yet achieved intentional communication, The Affective Communication Assessment (Coupe, J., Barton, L., Barber, M., Collins., Levy, D. and Murphy, D. 1985) provides ways to identify potentially communicative behaviours and the settings in which they are likely to occur.

The early sections of this document follow this developmental framework of functional communication, a process which is highly dependent on the quality and appropriateness of the response which the learner receives from the people and environment in which s/he lives and learns. Thus, for example a caregiver will accept any and all responses as meaningful from a baby of up to around six months but become much more selective in what is accepted as the infant is beginning to act intentionally. By doing so, the adult is now shaping intentional communication or reinforcing for the early learner the understanding that s/he can affect another's reactions by his/her behaviours and that some communicative gestures/ vocalisations are more effective than others. From then on the various purposes for which the learner uses his/her communicative strategies develop into more extensive and complex intentions (Harding 1983).

The effects of an impairment in one area of learning has consequences for the development in all others including the process of communication. Some of these consequences are considered by Fagg, Aherne, Skelton and Thornber (1990). Thus, for example, the development of prelingual communication is affected when mutual gaze and gesture are blocked by a visual impairment. An auditory impairment can also disrupt the communicative process. Apparent lack of responses by children with impairments can lead to impaired social relations which in turn compound the difficulty. The need for the earliest possible diagnosis of an impairment, followed by rapid intervention to minimise its handicapping effects is thus essential.

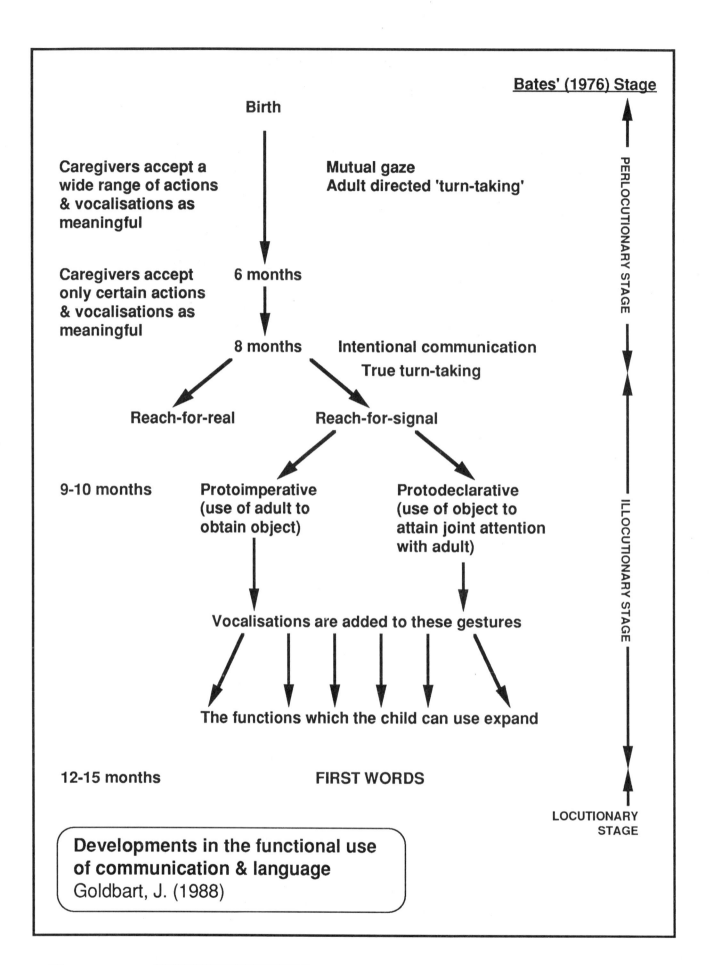

Bates' (1976) Stage

Birth

Caregivers accept a wide range of actions & vocalisations as meaningful

Mutual gaze
Adult directed 'turn-taking'

6 months

Caregivers accept only certain actions & vocalisations as meaningful

8 months

Intentional communication

True turn-taking

Reach-for-real   Reach-for-signal

9-10 months   Protoimperative (use of adult to obtain object)   Protodeclarative (use of object to attain joint attention with adult)

Vocalisations are added to these gestures

The functions which the child can use expand

12-15 months   FIRST WORDS

Developments in the functional use of communication & language
Goldbart, J. (1988)

PERLOCUTIONARY STAGE

ILLOCUTIONARY STAGE

LOCUTIONARY STAGE

Figure 1

Page *12*

Implications for Approaches to Programmes of Study

It is clear that the skills involved in the process of communication at any level cannot be taught or extended in isolation from a context which has meaning for the learner. This in turn is fundamental to the development of the interrelated elements of understanding/listening and expression. The quality of the interactions s/he is involved in is a crucial and integral part of this process. For these reasons **the approaches and activities used in teaching cannot be separated from the targeted skills and all of these aspects should facilitate child initiation and response in two way interaction. Hence this document does not separate attainment targets from programmes of study but combines the two in a process which is child centred.**

Rogers-Warren, Warren and Baer (1983) among others, suggest a change in teaching approach for children with developmental delay to reflect natural social and communicative interchanges in which;

• the learner must interact with the environment in order to have a context in which communication can take place.
• the learner must interact with the teacher in this communicative context. These exchanges should happen in a turn-taking way, focussing upon the interaction.

They suggest a 'conversation based language learning model' in an environment which

> *'contains persons who do not naturally respond to the child's lowered responsiveness but seek to increase responsiveness without becoming unusually directive of the child's behaviour'.*

Five recommendations are made to the teacher.

1. Follow the child's lead.
2. Assume the child is trying to communicate and accommodate these attempts in some appropriate way.
3. Make sure you always respond in some way to the child's attempt to communicate.
4. Only provide corrective feedback in a positive way.
5. Talk with the child, limiting instructions and directives.

Wood and colleagues (1986), in their analysis of conversational styles and the impact of these on the communication process for children with hearing difficulties, demonstrate the way teacher-talk influences the quality of the contribution made by the child. Their conclusion is also emphasised by Webster and Wood (1989):

> *'Children's spontaneous language flourishes when adults respond to what the child has to say....and avoid high control moves. It is the adult's input which ..sustains and engages the child as a language partner'.*

There are challenging and exciting implications for intervention in the development of communication for children with severe learning difficulties. Schaffer (1986) highlights the evolving perspective that:

> *'Human development is fundamentally a joint enterprise between child and caretakers'.*

and its implications that;

> *'Cognitive functions require a social context for their initial emergence and subsequent facilitation before they eventually become internalised as properties of individuals.'*

McConkey (1987) summarises three components of the social context of learning or the interactive approach. The first is expressed by Bruner (1972) as he describes the **dialogue** between the more experienced and the less experienced and the crucial role this two way flow has in the learning process.

The second attribute of the interactive process is highlighted by Vygotsky (1978) as the need for learning to be **meaningful** for children and

> *'incorporated into a task that is necessary and meaningful for life'.*

Lastly, Donaldson (1978) draws attention to the importance of the teacher facilitating a sense of satisfaction and **success** for the child by guiding him

> *'towards tasks where he will be able objectively to do well, but not too easily, not without putting forth some effort, not*

without difficulties to be mastered, errors to be overcome,
creative solutions to be found .'

McConkey observes that these components can be less emphasised in some teaching approaches which are

'teacher initiated, teacher-maintained activities with a high
dependency on rote repetition, prompting and extrinsic
reinforcement.'

He outlines some differences between interactive learning approaches and more prescriptive methods. Some aspects of the following points, extracted from the context of his more detailed discussion, may at first seem to be oversimplified characteristics of some prescriptive methods and because of this, unduly critical. However, they help us to reconsider our approach and to ensure that, as **we create the contexts and structure learning experiences with and for pupils, we are incorporating important elements of the interactive process and social context for learning.** In practice, the interactive approach calls for skillful structuring by the teacher.

Prescriptive	Interactive
Teacher initiates - child responds	Child initiates - teacher responds
Learning targets are based on a task analysis	Learning targets are based on a skills analysis
Context is secondary to teaching techniques	Meaningful contexts are essential
Focus is mainly upon abilities	Abilities are viewed in social and emotional contexts
Extrinsic reinforcers are encouraged	Intrinsic motivation emphasised

(Adapted from McConkey 1987)

Many of the published 'language teaching' programmes divorce language from the everyday interaction in which skills grow. Such programmes focus on teaching object labels and putting sounds, words and sentences together, in specific lessons. Behavioural techniques may be advocated to teach these skills. However, if these methods are used in an inflexible way, rather than being incorporated into a more interactive approach, there is little opportunity for meaningful exchanges or initiation by the child. The learner may also experience difficulty in generalising the use of skills into everyday situations. Language which does not communicate is lifeless. If the learning situation itself is prescribed out of the context of the learner's direct experience and interest, there is little intrinsic motivation to communicate. However it may be argued that there is still a place for reinforcing linguistic skills out of context, provided the child is able to know why it is happening.

Goldbart (1988b) summarises studies of classroom interactions which suggest that initiation by learners with severe learning difficulties are less frequent and less effective than non impaired peers. She suggests a reason for this:

> *'In many ways a 'well-run' classroom is not a good place to learn to communicate or affect your environment...children are provided with food at mealtimes, and a drink at breaktimes...children are not allowed to remain at one activity for too long.....*
>
> *What need is there to communicate?'*

Philosophical Considerations

Before considering what would constitute a well run class room in terms of strategies for enhancing communication through an interactive approach, it is important to also recognise the philosophical background to promoting functional communication and facilitating and responding to the initiations of all pupils.

As Banes (1990) points out, the interactive approach to the education of pupils with severe/profound learning difficulties reflects the principles of the growing self advocacy movement and its promotion of an increase in awareness of their basic human rights. Self advocacy includes activities such as legal actions and activities to secure rights. At the heart of the movement is the individual's human right to express needs and make decisions in everyday activities where opportunities for informed choice making, self direction and group participation are also a basic right.

Communication and decision-making skills are central to self advocacy. As a result of her extensive research into the area of self advocacy, Crawley (1988) found that skills related to communication and feelings of confidence were not addressed in training. She highlights these areas of need which should be met from the earliest possible age.

Cross Curricular Strategies Facilitating Communication

Most meaningful interactions take place in everyday exchanges in all the environments in which the pupil lives and learns, rather than in formal communication lessons. **Communication is a cross-curricular skill** and a process to be fostered by all those with whom the learner interacts (Curriculum Guidance 3 1990). The promotion of partnership with parents and interdisciplinary collaboration are of fundamental importance in ensuring the quality of these interactions. On-going assessment must also be made in collaboration with parents and where possible with the child him/herself.

Central to this process is ensuring that the learner develops a **means** of communicating which is understood, valued, sensitively interpreted by all concerned. It is also vital for the learner to have a reason or **purpose** to communicate. Providing stimulating, challenging and motivating activities which are satisfying for the learner but which call forth the need to communicate are crucial. These activities must include enabling the learner to discover that **communication is enjoyable and brings results**. Some general strategies which promote communication across the curriculum have been considered by Goldbart (1988b):

Giving the learner opportunities to:

- express real **choices**, needs or preferences
- refuse or request objects or events
- experience some unpredictable events or the nonoccurrence of normally reliable events in order to have a reason to comment on or communicate with others about something unexpected.
- solve problems as individuals and as a group member
- set up and participate in 'joint action routines' or interactive games and routines which involve turn-taking, experience in communicating in different roles and for different purposes (Snyder-Mclean et al,1984.)

Personal and social education, which incorporates the fostering of self esteem, positive relationships and social understanding, is a fundamental cross-curricular dimension. It is also fundamental to the development of effective communication. Facilitating and responding to the child's initiation and recognising the social and emotional contexts for learning are essential to this process, which is considered in practice in the following section of this document.

SECTION 2: Process of Communication in Practice

A Model for Learning

The diagram overleaf summarises the process of communication in which the learner participates actively during interactions. It adopts a cyclical model of learning which incorporates and begins with a meaningful context. The learner must first interact with the environment in this context, from which the motivation and reason to communicate arises; secondly, he/she must interact with another person(s) in this communicative context. In order to do so, intellectual, social and linguistic skills are drawn from to choose a communicative strategy. The interchanges which then take place occur in a turn taking fashion in which receptive and expressive skills are used, with interest focussing on the interaction itself and its purpose.

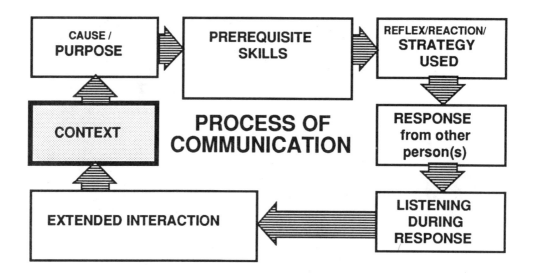

DEFINITIONS OF THE BOXES

Context: The 'functional' and meaningful situation the pupil is in, which gives rise to the *need* or *purpose* to communicate. Situations which are known to be motivating to the pupil and which are within his/her stage of understanding need to be created.

Purpose: The reason established by the *pupil* to obtain a desired outcome eg need satisfaction, seeking attention etc. At the early stages of development, before a purpose can be intentionally formed by the pupil, the adult interprets the reason for a reflex or reaction eg hunger, discomfort. In this case it is more of a *cause* of the communication than an intentional purpose.

Prerequisite skills: Skills the pupil already possesses and which are needed for interaction eg eye contact, gesture, single words, joint reference with object and person. These skills incorporate social, intellectual and linguistic abilities, at all stages of development.

Strategy used: The repertoire of behaviours selected by the *pupil* to establish a communicative interaction with another person(s) eg pointing, looking, vocalising, touching, banging objects etc. At the early stages of development these behaviours/ actions are *reflexes* or *reactions* which are interpreted by an adult as meaningful strategies eg increase in body movement, smile, frown etc.

Response: The reaction/feedback of the other person. A positive response indicates to the pupil that the strategy used has been successful and is the beginning of an extended two-way interaction. An inappropriate response may prevent further exchange.

Listening: Pupil's response during the other persons feedback eg stilling, eye contact, turn towards.

Extended Interaction: Two way exchange of words, actions, movements etc between pupil and other person(s) resulting from the response of the adult to the pupil and the pupil to the adult. A turn taking situation is developed and the adult allows for a *pause* after each interaction giving the pupil *time* to respond and valuing all the pupil's behaviours as communicative.

The first Statement of Attainment in English Speaking and Listening can be considered in the format of this model. The Attainment Target (Participate as Speaker and Listener in group activity) is incorporated naturally into the process. The example of this Attainment Target given in the National Curriculum document (playing the role of shop keeper) is the context and purpose for this particular interaction.

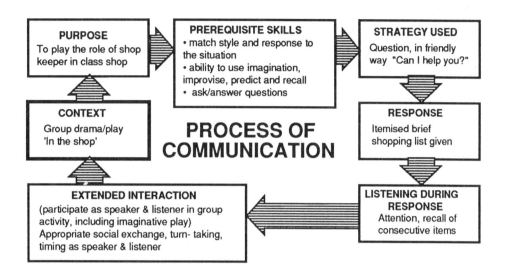

This document considers the process of communication, from the earliest experiences of interaction within Level 1 of the National Curriculum. The first five stages correspond to levels identified by various researchers in this field of learning, the initial three stages being at an early, preintentional level. These levels have been summarised by Coupe and Joliffe (1988) and are in the process of being validated for assessment purposes. The sixth stage, which includes the above example, is on going throughout the levels identified in the National Curriculum and indeed throughout adult life as people continue to develop skills in aspects of communication.

At each of the following stages, a list of resources for further reading to aid assessment and intervention will be given. The aim of this document is to provide an overview of the cross-curricular skill of communication, incorporating speaking and listening, as a framework for on-going curriculum development and complimentary assessment procedures. It is not the purpose to fully represent all the skills and concepts which the broad stages of this process should include. Instead exemplars of interactions and corresponding programmes of study at various stages are given with learners who have a diverse range of needs. A blank version of the diagrams used for these examplars is provided on the following page. It may be extended and tailor made by the teacher to meet the learner's individual needs and experiences in a wide range of learning contexts in and out of school.

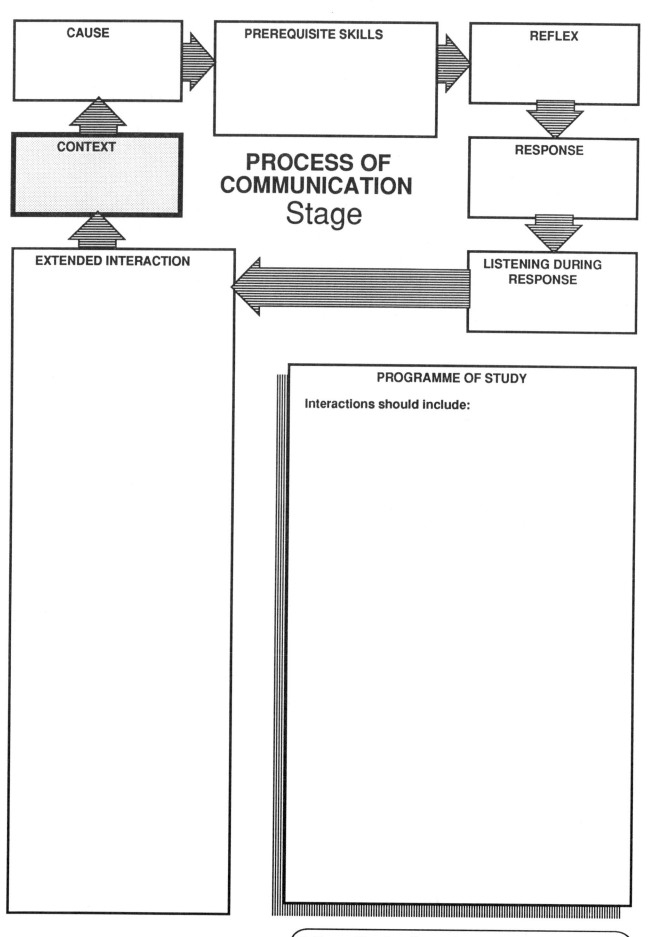

CAUSE

PREREQUISITE SKILLS

REFLEX

CONTEXT

PROCESS OF COMMUNICATION
Stage

RESPONSE

EXTENDED INTERACTION

LISTENING DURING RESPONSE

PROGRAMME OF STUDY

Interactions should include:

Process of Communication Stages 1 - 6 within Level 1 (including Programmes of Study & Attainment Target 1

CAUSE	**PREREQUISITE SKILLS**	**REFLEX**
Hunger	• reflex responses to own needs • can repeat some own body actions • cries, makes throaty noises • selective looking/orientation	Cry, stiffen

PROCESS OF COMMUNICATION
Stage 1

CONTEXT

Meal time
(smell of food)

RESPONSE

Comforts & feeds first spoonful of potato then pauses

LISTENING DURING RESPONSE

Quiets, stills, relaxes

EXTENDED INTERACTION

LEARNER: eye search, head up, mouth open.

ADULT: giving close eye contact in return, saying 'you want more' and giving another spoonful. Pause.

LEARNER: fleeting eye contact, relax, mouth and tongue activity.

ADULT: physical/eye contact in return saying 'more', giving spoonful......this time of carrot. Pause.

LEARNER: (after time to experience this taste) eyes open/close rapidly, body stiffens, mouth open.

ADULT: (giving close eye contact and physical reassurance) says 'ugh, you don't like carrots'. Gives spoonful of potatoes immediately. Pause.

LEARNER: fleeting eye contact, relax, mouth and tongue activity, throaty sounds.

ADULT: 'that's better, umm, more'.

Interaction continues with adult interpreting like/dislike behaviours.

(Eventually small amounts of carrot are accepted when well disguised in potato and gravy).

PROGRAMME OF STUDY

Interactions should include:

• Mutual orientation/eye contact, with sustained gaze; mutual touch/physical contact.

• Joint participation in which the learner is encouraged to be an active and responsive partner in the process of progressive interaction.

• Mutual enjoyment of the interaction which gives 'interest and delight' to the learner and teacher eg interactive 'games.'

• Turn-taking in a burst/pause pattern in which the learner has time to respond and the feedback is appropriate and rewarding to that particular individual.

• Use of voice, face and body in an animated way and imitation of the learner's sounds and facial expression.

• Sensitive phasing of time and rhythm, with the teacher's reaction being shaped by the learner's, thus facilitating the learner having some measure of control.

• Sensitive and objective interpretation of the learner's responses as meaningful eg like/dislike, and appropriate, consistent responses to their potentially communicative behaviours so that the latter increase, become stronger and more consistent.

EXTENDED PROGRAMME OF STUDY: Stage 1

Learning experiences should include :

• Coactive experiences with responsive adult to compensate for the consequences of multiple impairments on the development of the whole child eg movement (restricted by PH/Visual impairments) ; exploration of reactive environment.

• Time to experience, with reassuring adult, and systematically react to the various sensory stimuli inherent in routine events e.g. smells during feeding; the vibration of adult's throat during vocal interaction. These should include contrasting sensory experiences to elicit a diversity of strong and increasingly differentiating responses which are consistently respected and acted upon in every situation, thereby giving more control to the learner and developing early choice making skills.

• Specific stimulation of each sense in order to develop perceptual awareness and sensory and motor skills e.g. visual fixation / tracking from centre to side; voice / sound / vibration orientation; hand / arm movements; holding; oral desensitisation.

• Provision for a stimulating and responsive environment where the pupils slightest movement / vocalisation has an effect on the environment, a big reinforcement, whether or not responsive adult is present.

• Prompting, reinforcing and shaping random / reflex movements towards actions which produce interesting effects e.g. swiping action / movement to switch on projected light image / familiar music; leg kicking to splash.

Resources For Curriculum Development could include:

Brazelton, T. (1979) Evidence of communication in neonatal behavioural assessment. In M. Bullowa (ed) *Before Speech* , Cambridge University Press, Cambridge.

Coupe,J., Barton,L., Barber,M., Collins, L., Levy D. and Murphy,D. (1985) The Affective Communication Assessment.   Manchester Education Committee: Melland School.

Goldbart,J., (1988) Re-examining the Development of Early Communication in Coupe, J and Golbart, J., (eds) *Communication Before Speech.* Croom Helm. London.

Glenn, S. (1987) Interactive Approaches To Working With Children With Profound And Multiple Learning Difficulties. In B. Smith (ed) *Interactive Approaches to the Education of Children with Severe Learning Difficulties.* Westhill College. Birmingham.

Hewett, D. and Nind, M. (1987) Developing an Interactive Curriculum for Pupils with Severe and Complex Learning Difficulties: A Classroom Process. In B. Smith (ed)*Interactive Approaches to the Education of Children with Severe Learning Difficulties.*   Westhill College. Birmingham.

Longhorn, F., (1988) *Planning a Sensory Curriculum and Sensory Banks for the Very Special Child.* London. Souvenir Press.

Ouvry, C., (1987) *Educating Children with Profound Handicaps* (British Institute of Mental Handicap) Kidderminster.

CAUSE	PREREQUISITE SKILLS	REACTION

CAUSE

Enjoyment

PREREQUISITE SKILLS
- can make some actions on environment eg reaching/holding motivating objects/people
- can make some sounds eg aah

REACTION

Open mouth, smiles, head up

CONTEXT
During 1st game of repetitive, fun interaction .. being swung in air

PROCESS OF COMMUNICATION
Stage 2

RESPONSE
Adult repeats action, laughing with child and giving eye contact. Pauses

EXTENDED INTERACTION

ADULT: 'Again, Vicky? 1...2..' (semi swing)

LEARNER: open mouth, smile, head up, arm raised

ADULT: 'Three..ee' (twirling her right round in the air)

LEARNER: (during twirl) laughs out loud, head up

MUTUAL: eye contact,...laughing

ADULT: (after twirl and pause with mutual eye contact) 'Again, Vicky? 1......2......' Pause (after semi swing routine during '1..2')

LEARNER: open mouth, vocalisation, arm raised.

ADULT: 'Three....eee' (full twirl).

MUTUAL: eye contact, laughing.

LEARNER: (initiates after pause) arm up, vocalisation, smile.

ADULT: (quickly) '1...2..Three...eee.'

MUTUAL: smiling, eye contact and interaction, vocalisation ...turn taking interaction.

LISTENING DURING RESPONSE

Orientates towards adult Attentive, brief eye contact

PROGRAMME OF STUDY

Interactions should include:

All the components of POS Stage 1 and in addition;

- Teacher waits for increasing vocalisation eg open vowels, plosives and voluntary head/arm movement (the learner's identified repertoire of liking behaviours).

- Tone of adult voice/facial expression is increasingly important and responded to, eg in anticipation of exciting event, with learner developing more facial expressions.

- Enabling the learner to actively maintain the interaction.

- Opportunity for learner to initiate with more consistency and frequency.

- Facilitating more discriminating responses to a wider range of stimuli, which are responded to appropriately in all the contexts in which the individual lives and learns.

- Creating repeated and motivating actions/events which always have the same result in order to learn to anticipate outcomes and use procedure as a causal action eg repetitive games, consistent environmental clues.

EXTENDED PROGRAMME OF STUDY: Stage 2

Learning experiences should include opportunities to:

• <u>develop new and differentiating schemes</u> to reproduce interesting events with objects as well as people e.g. hitting, mouthing, physical exploration, looking when holding.

• <u>develop skills in visually examining and reaching for objects</u>eg grasping objects, shaping hand in anticipation, looking at held object and turning it over / around.

• <u>develop potentially communicative repertoire in choice making</u>, which is responded to selectively and consistently by adults in everyday situations, to shape pupils towards intentional communication eg preferential reactions to one sensory stimulus from another, with an increasingly wider range of stimuli experienced.

• <u>use 'dialogue' of sound / action</u> with adults to encourage eventual initiation of interaction with adults / peers and imitation of sound / gestures.

• <u>consolidate the concept of cause and effect</u> by facilitating a reactive environment eg through varied switch systems to activate motivating effects, eg familiar taped voices. Alternative means of operating these switches should be used eg finer head/arm movements, sounds.

• <u>search for sound source,</u> especially vocalisation.

• <u>have line of regard / orientation</u> followed by adult and learn to respond to latter's gaze direction, movement.

Resources For Curriculum Development could include:

As in Stage I and:
Brinker, R. P. and Lewis, M. (1982) Discovering the competent handicapped infant: a process approach to assessment and intervention. *Topics in Early Childhood Special Education, 2* 1-16

Jaffe, J. Stern, D. and Peery, J. (1987) Conversational coupling of gaze behaviour in prelinguistic human development. *Journal of Psycholinguistic Research*, 2, 321-9.

McConkey, R. (1987) Interaction: The Name of the Game. In B. Smith (ed) *Interactive Approaches to the Education of Children with Severe Learning Difficulties.* Westhill College. Birmingham.

Owens, R. (1988) (2nd Ed.) *Language Development : an introduction*. Charles Merrill, Columbus, Ohio.

Trevarthen, C. (1979) Communication and co-operation in early infancy: a description of primary inter-subjectivity. In Bullowa (ed), *Before Speech* . Cambridge University Press. Cambridge.

CAUSE	PREREQUISITE SKILLS	REACTION

CAUSE

(Interpreted)
want the instrument

PREREQUISITE SKILLS
• intentional and more complex actions on environment
• object permanence
• use of various tones, sounds (consonants, vowels) and babble
• can terminate interaction

REACTION

Bangs table with hand

CONTEXT

In music session
(group in a circle)

PROCESS OF COMMUNICATION
Stage 3

RESPONSE

Adult goes close,
giving eye contact

EXTENDED INTERACTION

ADULT: tapping keys on electronic organ, 'Do you want this, Philip?'

LEARNER: moves his hand towards the organ, smiling.

ADULT: taps it again and repeats, excitedly ' Do you want this Philip?'

LEARNER: touches the organ, laughing.

ADULT: (waiting for vocalisation) still holding and tapping it repeats, animatedly, 'Do you want it?'

LEARNER: vocalises loudly, giving eye contact.

ADULT: immediately gives it and begins to sing learner's favourite song.

JOINT INTERACTION: involving the electronic organ and vocalising in song which has a repetitive refrain. The song also contains pauses, anticipated outcomes and opportunities for learner to initiate.

LISTENING DURING RESPONSE

Stops banging,
moves towards adult,
smiles on eye contact

PROGRAMME OF STUDY

Interactions should include:

• interpretation of learners behaviour as an intention to carry out an action and as trying to find out about something.

• teacher being increasingly selective in those behaviours responded to and thus reinforced eg vocalisation more valued in communicative terms than hand/head movement. (Vocalisations include repeated and new consonants and vowels and varying pitch, tone volume).

• 'dialogue' which follows set routines of interaction, with the emphasis more on toys/objects which are motivating to the learner. These routines incorporate joint attention and action and facilitate the learner being able to anticipate interesting and exciting events.

• opportunities for the learner to repair and terminate interaction as an equal partner.

• encouraging the learner to derive meaning from and differentially respond to the teacher's intonation patterns, voice quality and facial expression; adult responding to learner's tone expressing varied emotions.

• shared attention of learner and adult on person(s), object(s) and events close by.

• encouraging learner's use of a more sophisticated, broken pattern of eye contact rather than sustained gaze.

• increased initiation by learner, with the adult creating the opportunities.

EXTENDED PROGRAMME OF STUDY: Stage 3

Learning experiences should include opportunities to:

• search for and locate sound source to side and below ear level.

• repair an interaction which adult or learner has closed.

• further develop ways of acting upon the objects/people in environment eg hand transference, shake, explore, visually directed reaching, switches operating wide range of motivating effects, objects.

• further develop turn taking skills, acting on adult or object, use actions at same time as adult.

• use strategies to achieve a desired end result, coordinating hand/eye skills eg drops object to reach for another wanted object, orientates self towards source of motivating stimulus (brought into edge of auditory / visual field) whilst already engaged on other; extend visual tracking skills.

• develop socially instigated actions eg follows the point / gesture of another person to an object / event close by.

• experience displacement of objects to establish the concept of object permanence e.g. look for falling objects.

• vocalise to self, reflection, people, music, objects and responding to commands with environmental sounds in context.

Resources For Curriculum Development could include:

As Stages 1 and 2 and :

Harding, C. G. (1983) Setting the stage for language acquisition: Communication development in the first year. In R. Golinkoff (ed) *The Transition from Prelinguistic to Linguistic Communication.* Laurence Erlbaum, Hillsdale New Jersey.

Glenn, S.M. and Cunningham, C.C. (1984) Special Care but Active Learning. *Special Education Forward Trends, 11* 33-36

Harding, C. G. and Golinkoff, R. (1980) The origins of intentional vocalisations in prelinguistic infants. *Child Development, 49,* 33-40

Kiernan, C. and Reid, B (1987) *The Preverbal Communication Schedule* (PVCS), N.F.E.R./Nelson. Windsor.

Kiernan, C., Reid, B. and Goldbart, J. (1987) *Foundations of Communication and Language.* Manchester University Press. Manchester.

PURPOSE

Desire for mechanical toy to be activated

PREREQUISITE SKILLS

- intentional communication
- causality
- joint reference with object & person
- vocalisations
- some use of gesture
- turn taking

STRATEGY USED

Goes to adult, touches adult's arm. Looks at adult and puts car in adult's hand

CONTEXT

In classroom

PROCESS OF COMMUNICATION
Stage 4.1

RESPONSE

Adult looks at car, looks at learner and says ' Oh yes, a car '

EXTENDED INTERACTION

ADULT: looks at learner and asks 'should I put the car away?' Pause. Walks towards toy box.
LEARNER: follows adult, pulls adults arm, looks at adult, frowns and takes car off adult.
ADULT: looks at toy box and says 'No?' and asks 'What should we do then?'
LEARNER: looks at adult, puts car in adults hand, stamps feet with agitation and vocalises.
ADULT: looks puzzled at learner with hands out stretched and asks 'what should I do with the car ?'
LEARNER: puts adults other hand over car, vocalises and gestures 'Go'.
ADULT: looks at learner, smiles and says 'Ah, car go'. Winds up car and gives to learner.
LEARNER: puts car on floor, lets go squeals/laughs and looks at adult.
ADULT: says 'whee'.
LEARNER: looks at adult and points to car and says 'eee'.
ADULT: looks at child and asks 'again?' Pause.
LEARNER: vocalises with agitated excitement.
ADULT: looks at learner and says 'OK, go and get the car then'.
LEARNER: runs and gets the car and places in adults hand.

LISTENING DURING RESPONSE

Learner puts adults other hand over car and vocalises

PROGRAMME OF STUDY Stage 4
Interactions should include:

- initiating communication/interactions with adults and peer group in naturally occurring situations.

- engaging in formulated routines for joint attention with adult and later groups of peers eg through everyday activities such as washing the dishes, meal times, shopping and home corner play etc.

- developing strategies in turn taking.

- establishing joint reference of self and a person with an object, event or other person eg communicates to adult the sight/sound of aeroplane in the sky.

- using vocal and/or physical repertoire of behaviours to get a person to create/provide events and actions eg to push a jack in the box down, to switch on radio/cassette.

- producing physical and vocal messages to convey request, greeting etc.

- using vocalisations plus actions to gain attention / object / event.

- intentionally using eye contact and movement towards a desired goal eg takes adult to milk crate.

- communicating intentionally with gestures, vocalisations and protowords.

- gaining attention for the purpose of communicating.

EXTENDED PROGRAMME OF STUDY: Stage 4.1

Learning experiences should include opportunities to:

• express *real* choices, needs or preferences throughout the day eg milk or squash?, straw or cup?, tea or coffee?, pen or pencil?.

• request *and* refuse objects and events eg the need to use the toilet.

• comment or communicate with others about something unexpected eg non occurrence of normally reliable events/routines eg no chairs in classroom, no shoe after PE lesson, no lead for kettle.

• solve real life problems both individually and in groups eg how to obtain an object which is within sight but out of reach, how to take a square table through the classroom door.

• experience a variety of ways of obtaining a desired environmental event eg use of supports, switches and for someone with multiple disabilities, communication with an adult who then acts as an agent.

• understand and express the desire for 'more' and 'no more' in context.

• 'use' adult to gain an object or event and use the latter to gain adult attention. Adult prompts through gesture and situational clues.

Resources For Curriculum Development could include:

• Coupe, J. and Jolliffe, J. (1988) An Early Communication Curriculum: Implications for Practice. In Coupe, J. and Goldbart, J. (Eds.) *Communication Before Speech.* Croom Helm. London.

• Goldbart, J. (1988) Communication for a Purpose. In Coupe, J. and Goldbart, J.(Eds.) *Communication Before Speech.* Croom Helm. London.

• Harris, J. (1987) Interactive Styles for Language Facilitation.   In Smith, B. (Ed.)*Interactive Approaches to the Education of Children with Severe Learning Difficulties.* Westhill College. Birmingham.

• Kiernan, C. and Reid, B. (1987) *The Pre - Verbal Communication Schedule.* NFER/Nelson. Windsor.

• Snyder-McLean, L., Solomonson, B., McLean, J. and Sack, S. (1984) Structuring joint action routines: a strategy for facilitating communication and language development in the classroom. *Seminars in Speech and Language.* 5, 213-28.

PURPOSE

Wants to ride the bike.

CONTEXT
Playground.
Another pupil riding a
bike in the distance.

PRE REQUISITE SKILLS
• fleeting eye contact.
• knows adult will assist in fulfilling a request.
• can use words which are largely comprised of immediate or delayed echolalia.

PROCESS OF COMMUNICATION
Stage 4.2

STRATEGY USED
Hovering stance nearby, but not facing adult.
Loud noises and shouts.
Self injurious behaviour.

RESPONSE
Adult physically turns learner towards her.
Holds hands firmly.
Initiates pause whilst learner calms.

LISTENING DURING RESPONSE
Cessation of self injurious behaviour.
Agitated bodily movements.

EXTENDED INTERACTION

ADULT: 'What do you want?'
LEARNER: 'Want to go to Blackpool lights.' (repeated several times.)
ADULT: ignores learners speech.
(Interpreted as anxiety and desire to make a request.)
Points to learner's pocket.
LEARNER: follows point. Takes mini photo album out of pocket.
ADULT: holds hand out to receive.
LEARNER: gives album to adult.
ADULT: prompts learner to look at and point to each photograph in turn.
LEARNER: gives intermittent eye contact to adult. Points to each photograph. Says 'No thank you toilet.' 'No thank you swing.'Yes thank you bike.'
ADULT: Holds album out to learner.
LEARNER: Receives album and replaces in pocket.
ADULT: 'Where's the bike?'
LEARNER: Echoes 'where's the bike?' in exactly same tone as adult. Looks towards bike.
ADULT: Walks with pupil to bike. Says ' What do you want?'
LEARNER: 'Yes thank you bike.'
ADULT: Prompts learner to gain attention of pupil on bike, by tapping pupil on shoulder.
LEARNER: Taps pupil on shoulder.
ADULT: Models phrase 'Can I have a go on the bike?'
LEARNER: Faces other pupil and models phrase as stated, in same intonation as adult.
2ND. PUPIL: (says to learner) 'Okay Paul, your turn.' and walks away.
LEARNER: 'Okay Paul, your turn. Have the bike in a minute.' Then rides away.

PROGRAMME OF STUDY

Interactions should include:

• Adult interpretation of negative behaviour and emotions as expressive communication.

• Adult interpretation of some immediate and delayed echolalic speech as potentially meaningful and interactive. Recognition that some regular phrases occur in similar contexts eg when learner appears to convey confusion, anxiety, distress or frustration. Recognition that learner may resort to echolalia as a substitute for lack of understanding, or when unsure of how to use any strategy to communicate.

• Gradual and natural progression from minimal emphasis on interpersonal contact eg eye contact to greater interactive exchange. This is more likely to increase during an activity rather than worked for in isolation.

• Shared understanding of the use of simple gesture. (eg pointing.)

• Use of physical contact to gain attention eg tap on shoulder.

• Modelling appropriate physical stance during social interactions eg turning towards other participant.

• Modelling appropriate phrases in functional contexts.

• Joint reference and attention. Exchanges involving giving and receiving objects.

EXTENDED PROGRAMME OF STUDY: Stage 4.2
Learning experiences should include opportunities to:

The programme of study presents as similar to that in Stage 4.1. However it is thought necessary to give a brief summary of this pupil, who clearly experiences complex difficulties in the understanding and use of interactive and communicative strategies.

The pupil has a condition known as Autism, the characteristics of which create obstacles for him which influence his ability to make sense of social interactions and relationships. Many of his difficulties are reflected in Case Study 2, 'Lorna' in _Entitlement For All In Practice._ (1990. Fagg S. Aherne P. Skelton S. Thornber A.) The implications for access to relevant personal and curricular experiences are also considered.

In the area of English (Communication), this pupil presents as a child with all the basic tools for using language. The fact that he can speak, however, gives little indication of his ability to communicate, and can mask his severe comprehension problems. His speech consists largely of immediate or delayed echolalia, ie instant or recalled repetition of other peoples' speech, which may either be spoken as first heard or with poor control of pitch, volume and intonation of voice. He needs immense support to assist him to understand, interpret and use speech as a communication tool, in conjunction with alternative or accompanying non verbal means. He also needs to practise activities which promote and motivate him to come into contact and interact with others, thus forming relationships.

Resources For Curriculum Development could include:

• Fay, W.H. and Schuler, A. L. (1980)_Emerging Language in Autistic Children: Language Intervention Series._ Series Editor, Schiefelbusch, Richard L. Edward Arnold.

• The Association of Headteachers of Autistic Children and Adults. (1985) _The Special Curricular Needs of Autistic Children._ National Autistic Society.

• Jordon, R. and Powell, S.(1990) _The Special Needs of Autistic Children: Learning And Thinking Skills._ The Association of Headteachers of Autistic Children and Adults. National Autistic Society.

• Wing, L. undated _The Handicaps of Autistic Children: An aid to diagnosis._ National Autistic Society.

• Kiernan, C. and Reid, B. (1987) _The Pre-Verbal Communication Schedule._ NFER/Nelson. Windsor

PURPOSE

Desire to give out milk

PREREQUISITE SKILLS

- intentional communication
- means end
- joint reference with object & person
- gesture/signs
- some single words

STRATEGY USED

Pulls adults arm, points to milk crate, signs 'drink' and says 'rink'..

PROCESS OF COMMUNICATION
Stage 5

CONTEXT

Milk break

RESPONSE

Adult tells learner to get himself a bottle of milk.

LISTENING DURING RESPONSE

Learner looks at adult, points to classmates and asks 'rink?'.

EXTENDED INTERACTION

ADULT: holds up milk bottle and asks 'who would like to give out the milk?'
LEARNER: looks at adult, points to self and says 'me'.
ADULT: hands straws and cups to learner and requests that each pupil choose which they want to drink with.
LEARNER: hands out milk to first classmate, gives eye contact and says 'here'. Places straws and cups in front and asks 'which want?'.
(Classmate selects straw.)
LEARNER: hands out milk to second classmate and asks 'which want?' after placing straws and cups in front.
CLASSMATE: pushes straws and cups away.
LEARNER: puts straws and cups in front of classmate and repeats 'you want?' in louder voice.
CLASSMATE: pushes straws and cups away and turns back on learner.
LEARNER: picks up cup and straws, moves round to face classmate, stares at classmate, stamps foot and asks 'which want?' in raised voice.
CLASSMATE: looks the other way and shakes head.
LEARNER: gives milk bottle to classmate.
CLASSMATE: pushes bottle away, shakes head, goes to sink and reaches for tap.
LEARNER: goes to classmate, touches arm and takes to table. Gets cup, fills with water and gives to classmate.
CLASSMATE: takes straw and drinks water.

PROGRAMME OF STUDY

Interactions should include :

- initiating and controlling for the outcome of a situation eg during milk/coffee breaks, preparing for dinner time etc.

- repairing a misunderstanding non verbally eg by repetition, rephrasing with different pitch or gesture, giving more information etc.

- joining in turn taking sequences with adults and peer group eg games, everyday routines.

- requesting and giving information and rejecting objects, events or people in functionally appropriate situations.

- communicating intentionally with gestures, vocalisations and protowords.

- using objects appropriately and functionally eg puts straw in bottle, coffee in mug, cup on saucer etc.

- developing a variety of strategies to initiate an exchange eg proximity, eye contact, vocalisation etc.

- maintaining the topic and conversation by extending the interchange eg through question and answer, statement and reply.

EXTENDED PROGRAMME OF STUDY: Stage 5

Learning experiences should include opportunities to:

• communicate a range of meanings concerning people, objects and events which are familiar eg existence of entities, non existence of items usually expected, disappearance of things etc.

• be involved in simple events which clearly exemplify specific meanings which can then be sequenced to provide a meaningful routine eg activating toys, hiding objects, observing the location of objects.

• process information from situationally cued words eg 'put your coat on' said when standing next to the clothes peg at home time, 'wash your hands' said when standing next to the sink before dinner.

• convey new or changing aspects of their environment whilst assuming the listener has access to certain background information.

• communicate about their work and be encouraged to think about it.

• predict certain events which have an either/or outcome and communicate about them eg it will get dark, if you go swimming you will get wet.

• query/reflect on and communicate about work done eg attempts to rectify problem situation by communicating their enquiry.

• copy, anticipate and communicate about everyday patterns in self help routines / sequences eg dressing, teeth cleaning, washing etc.

Resources For Curriculum Development could include:

• Bates, E. (1976) *Language and Context: The Acquisition of Pragmatics.* Academic Press. New York.

• Coupe, Barton and Walker. (1988) Teaching First Meanings. In Coupe, J. and Goldbart, J. (Eds.) *Communication Before Speech.* Croom Helm. London.

• Goldbart, J. (1988) Communication for a Purpose. In Coupe, J. and Goldbart, J. (Eds.) *Communication Before Speech.* Croom Helm. London.

• Halliday, M.A.K. (1975) *Learning How To Mean: Explorations in the Development of Language.* Edward Arnold.

• Harris, J. (1987) Interactive Styles for Language Facilitation. In Smith, B. (Ed.) *Interactive Approaches to the Education of Children with Severe Learning Difficulties.* Westhill College. Birmingham.

• Knowles, W. and Masidlover, M. (1982) *Derbyshire Language Scheme.* Private Publication. Ripley, Derbyshire.

PURPOSE
Desire to know why the teacher was absent yesterday.

PREREQUISITE SKILLS

- intentional communication
- clear gestures and signs
- 2 and 3 word utterances

STRATEGY USED
Signs/says 'where you yesterday?'

CONTEXT
Registration

PROCESS OF COMMUNICATION
Stage 6.1

RESPONSE
Adult says/signs to learner 'I was away'.

LISTENING DURING RESPONSE
Learner looks at adult and sign/says 'Why?'

EXTENDED INTERACTION

ADULT: looks at pupil and says/signs 'I felt ill'.
LEARNER: looks at adult and signs/says 'were you sick?'
ADULT: looks at pupil and the class and says/signs 'I had a migraine. Do you know what a migraine is?'
CLASSMATE: 'My mum gets that.
ADULT: directs question at learner signs/says 'what is a migraine?'
LEARNER: shakes head, shrugs shoulders.
ADULT: continues to look at learner with questioning expression, signs/says 'Don't you know?'
LEARNER: says 'no' and casts eyes at table.
ADULT: says/signs 'never mind Jane I will tell you', pause to regain eye contact with the learner. 'A migraine is a very bad headache and sometimes it makes you sick as well.' After a pause directs question at class mate 'What does your mother do when she has a migraine?'
CLASSMATE: 'takes tablet.'
ADULT: to learner says/signs 'do you ever get a headache?'
LEARNER: 'no, me sick.'
ADULT: signs/says 'what makes you sick?'
LEARNER: signs/says 'lot ice cream'.
ADULT: smiles .

PROGRAMME OF STUDY Stage 6
Interactions should include:

- initiating and pursuing a question.

- answering questions and clarifying initial response.

- participating in questioning initiated by another person.

- developing intervention strategies to allow participation in an ongoing conversation.

- participating in response to questions directed at a group.

- presenting communication in alternative manner if response not understood eg use of signing to support verbal communication, use of alternative words or extension of initial response.

- using gesture and body language to assist the continuation of communicative exchanges.

- communication about activity or work being participated in.

- extending of social abilities connected with communication eg change of eye focus / body posture at different phases in the interaction, the consistent use of please and thank you.

- repairing misunderstandings by offering further information about the issue.

- negotiating over motivating issues eg why permission to have the tape recorder on should be given.

EXTENDED PROGRAMME OF STUDY: Stage 6.1

Learning experiences should include opportunities to:

• role play in different classroom or school learning areas eg hairdressers, cafe, post office, home corner.

• question freely eg at the beginning and end of the more formal learning sessions.

• find out information from another pupil or adult, using functional and drama/play situations.

• hypothesise and predict about possible answers to questions raised.

• extend their questions or answers to enhance the detail of their communication.

• know who may be able to answer certain questions eg ask member of supermarket staff where to find margarine.

• think about a question asked and if answer unknown seek answer by enquiry - verbal, utilisation of resources, previous experience recalled.

• participate in motivating situations that extend the contexts for communication eg educational visits, learning opportunities in different class groups (integration), live music/art sessions with professionals.

• attempt to solve problem situations set up by adult which require more complex strategies eg no cups for drinks, be encouraged to communicate their difficulty.

Resources For Curriculum Development could include:

• Bruner, J. (1983) *Child's Talk.* Oxford: Oxford University Press.

• Crystal, D. (1986) *Child language learning and linguistics.* E. Arnold. London.

• Knowles, W. and Masidlover, M.(1982) *Derbyshire Language Scheme.* Ripley, Derbyshire.

• DES (1989) *The Education of Children Under Five.*

• DES (1990) *The Teaching and Learning of Language and Literacy.* HMSO. London.

• Manchester City Council (1988) *Early Literacy Project.* Manchester: Manchester Education Committee.

• Manchester City Council (1989), *English National Curriculum, Key stage one.* Pankhurst Press. Manchester.

• NCC (1989) *A Curriculum for All.* NCC. York.

• Wood, D. (1988) *How Children Think and Learn.* Blackwell. London.

PURPOSE

To play the role of shop keeper in class shop

PREREQUISITE SKILLS

• match style and response to the situation
• ability to use imagination, improvise, predict and recall
• ask/answer questions

STRATEGY USED

Question, in friendly way "Can I help you?"

CONTEXT

Group drama/play 'In the shop'

PROCESS OF COMMUNICATION
Stage 6.2
English AT1 Speaking & Listening Level 1

RESPONSE

Itemised brief shopping list given

EXTENDED INTERACTION

(Participate as speaker and listener in group activity, including imaginative play)
Appropriate social exchange, turn taking, timing as speaker and listener.
RAZAK: 'Samosa please'.
HAZEL: 'Here you are, 20p.'
RAZAK: hands money over, gives eye contact and questioning expression looking at the till.
HAZEL: 'Your change.'
SUSHMA: 'Two bottles of milk'. (Says and signs speech not clear.)
HAZEL: '50p.'
RAZAK: looks on.
SUSHMA: 'Come my house .... drink.' (Signs and says)
HAZEL: 'I can't leave the shop.'
SUSHMA: looking at Razak 'You come.'
RAZAK: nods head and says 'Yes'.
HAZEL: 'Can you hear van?' All look out of shop area.
HAZEL: 'I am expecting a delivery.'
RAZAK: 'Can't see anything'.
SUSHMA: gestures 'Come on'.
RAZAK AND SUSHMA leave the shop area, RAZAK waves.
ADULT: comes into shop 'What can I buy for tea, Grandad is coming?'
HAZEL: 'What about fish fingers?'
ADULT: 'Grandad doesn't eat fish.'
HAZEL: 'Oh.' After a pause 'What about a Pizza?'
ADULT: 'Yes, please can I have two pizzas. How much will that be?'
HAZEL: 'A pound .' Gives Pizzas to the adult.
ADULT: 'Thank you.'

LISTENING DURING RESPONSE

Attention, recall of consecutive items

PROGRAMME OF STUDY: AT 1

Interactions should include:

• working with adults and pupils- involving discussion with others; listening to, and giving weight to , the opinions of others; perceiving the relevance of contributions: adjusting and adapting to views expressed;

• development of listening (and, as appropriate, reactive) skills in non-reciprocal situations, *eg radio programmes;*

• development of speaking and listening skills, both when role-playing and otherwise - when describing experiences, expressing opinions, articulated personal feelings and formulating and making appropriate responses to increasingly complex instructions and questions;

• development, by informal means and in the course of purposeful activities, of pupils' powers of concentration, grasp of turn-taking, ability to gain and hold the attention of their listeners, and ability to voice disagreement courteously with an opposing point of view.'

Extract from *English in the National Curriculum* (1989) programmes of study Key Stage 1.

Many pupils will support their verbal communication by gesture, signing, body language and the use of specialist aids.

EXTENDED PROGRAMME OF STUDY: AT 1

Learning experiences should include opportunities to:

• listen and respond to stories, rhymes, poems and songs familiar and unfamiliar. These should include examples from different cultures and authors and from the pupils' own work.

• securing responses to visual and aural stimuli, *eg pictures, television, radio, computer, telephone,* making use of audio and video recordings as appropriate.

• discussions of their work with other pupils and the teacher.

• collaborative planning of activities in a way which requires pupils to speak and listen.

• talking about experiences in or out of school, *eg a school trip, a family outing, a television programme seen.*

• telling stories and reciting poems that have been learnt by heart.

• collaborative and exploratory play.

• imaginative play and improvised drama:

• giving and receiving simple explanations, information and instructions; asking and answering questions.

Extract from English in the National Curriculum (1989) programmes of study key stage 1

Resources For Curriculum Development could include:

Crystal, D. (1986) *Listen to Your Child.* Hammersmith: Penguin.
DES (1990) *The Teaching and Learning of Language and Literacy.* London: HMSO.
Early Years Curriculum Group (1989) *The Early Years Curriculum and The National Curriculum.* Trentham Books.
Language and Learning (formerly GNOSIS). Questions. Publishing Company: Birmingham.
Jeffree, D.M. (1986) *Let Me to Speak.* London: Human Horizon Series, Souvenir Press.
MEC (1989) *English National Curriculum.* Manchester: Pankhurst Press.
NCC (1989) *English Key Stage 1 Non-Statutory Guidelines.*
NOP TALK The Journal of the National Oracy Project.
NOP (1990) Teaching Talking and Learning in Key Stage 1. York: NCC.
Smith, B. Ed (1990) *Interactive Approaches to the Education of Children with Severe Learning Difficulties.* Birmingham: Westhill College.
Tough, J. (1981) *A Place for Talk.* London: Ward Lock Educational.

Conclusion

We are becoming increasingly aware of the nature and quality of everyday interactions between adults and children and between children themselves. From the earliest stage of understanding, aspects of communication, including speaking and listening, develop progressively through dynamic exchanges in situations which are meaningful for the learner. Such situations often need to be skillfully created by the adult and ensuring the quality of interactions is no less challenging.

Mittler (1988) summarises some of the questions this document has begun to address:

> *How many interactions, whether verbal or non verbal are initiated by the child? Who responds and how? With what result? How can we provide each child with opportunities for choice and decision making? How can we help a child to learn that initiations of interaction are rewarding and lead to desired outcomes? Are there dangers in a well run school such that we might unwittingly deprive a child of such opportunities? Can individual educational programmes allow children to affect or even control the structure of the day? In our concern with teaching objectives, have we left space for children to influence their own curriculum?*

The answers can only be fully worked out by practising teachers in collaboration with all those concerned with the education of their pupils. The principle of teaching in a more natural environment in the context of everyday encounters and cross-curricular activities is a challenge to us all. It calls for continued commitment to incorporating the National Curriculum into the meaningful learning experiences often reflected in schools' existing curricula. It also calls for greater partnership with parents.

The art of effective communication is valued highly in all walks of life. As adults, we continue to learn more about the communicative process through our everyday contacts with others. Perhaps we need to be more sensitive to the non verbal ways in which we all communicate and so learn to appreciate more fully the alternatives to speech used by some of us.

Appendices

Citizenship
(Attainment Targets & Programmes of Study within Level 1 have been broken down)

Joe is 6 years old and has profound and multiple learning difficulties, which, for him, means that he is at a very early sensorimotor stage of understanding, compounded by severe physical and sensory impairments. He is as yet completely dependent upon other people for his needs and for most of his interactions with his environment. The overall aims of his curriculum include motivating and enabling him to have more control over his physical and social environment. Since Joe cannot speak or use recognised signs, his personal communicative strategies must be identified, acted upon and developed at all times. Giving him the time and opportunity to learn to make choices and to communicate preferences is an essential aspect of this process which is fundamental in education for citizenship.

SCIENCE PoS & AT1
Joe will
1 (a) systematically respond to sensory experiences inherent in routine events (AT 3)
2 (a) respond differentially to contrasting sensory stimulation as he learns to discriminate between them (these responses are potentially communicative and are followed up as in English)

PHYSICAL
Joe will
1. (a) maintain head control while sitting in motivating activity
(b) receive much coactive movement & experience.

MATHS PoS AT 1 & 9
Joe will
1 (a) make hand / finger contact with rewarding object.
(b) respond to this experience, eg - facial expression.
(c) repeat this through random actions, anticipating outcome.

WHAT
To develop choice-making and communication skills throughout the interrelated curriculum areas

HOW
• In a Cross-Curricular way in naturally occurring & motivating contexts, in group / individual situations. Time for specific skill learning / therapy is also essential.
• The style of teaching complements Joe's personal preferences being both coactive & interactive, positive, reassuring & fun, while including some behavioural techniques.

WHERE
At school & home, thus generalising learning to all Joe's situations, eg - breaks, lunchtimes, journeys.

ENGLISH PoS AT1
Joe will
1 respond differently to stimuli / experiences which adult interprets as like / dislike & consistently acts upon, eg - bodily relaxing / stiffening, eye contact / turn away.
2 take turns during social interaction, adult being selective re response accepted to encourage more communication eg eye contact, mouth open / smile for 'more' or head down for 'no more'.

GEOGRAPHY & HISTORY
Joe will
1 coactively experience his surroundings, which should be responsive to his movements towards exploration. His feelings and responses must be valued communicatively
2 experience a measure of set routines helping him feel time & to anticipate events in a secure atmosphere

CREATIVE ARTS
Joe will
1 coactively experience and give preferential responses to a variety of substances, textures & colours using his hands, feet & whole body
2 Listen to and express preferences between a variety of sung and instrumental music and movement

The skills leading to choice-making & communication are fundamental to all the cross-curricular themes for Joe & indeed for all pupils at different stages of understanding.

INFORMAL CURRICULUM
Breaktimes - Joe will taste two different drinks and be given time to give like/dislike responses which will consistently be acted upon
Lunchtimes - Joe will be given the various food items separately and his responses acted upon (various sauces may be tried to make school dinner more inviting!)
Leisure time - Joe will experience varied activities and situations, with his preferential responses being respected, enabling him to realise he can control events more

TECHNOLOGY
Supporting skills across the curriculum in enabling Joe to have more control over his environment
Joe will
1 reach towards touch screen - visual / sound reward.
2 use tilt switch on head to operate visual / auditory / vibratory stimuli of his preference.
3 hit switch to effect sound / vision - also electronic key board.

Appendix 1
(Aherne 1990)

Page 44

CROSS CURRICULAR PLANNING SHEET
TOPIC Interactions & Relationships

Class Team — Ms Syddall, Mr Ellis, Mrs Bateman

Individual / Group/class _Lorna_

Half Term / **Term** _Summer_

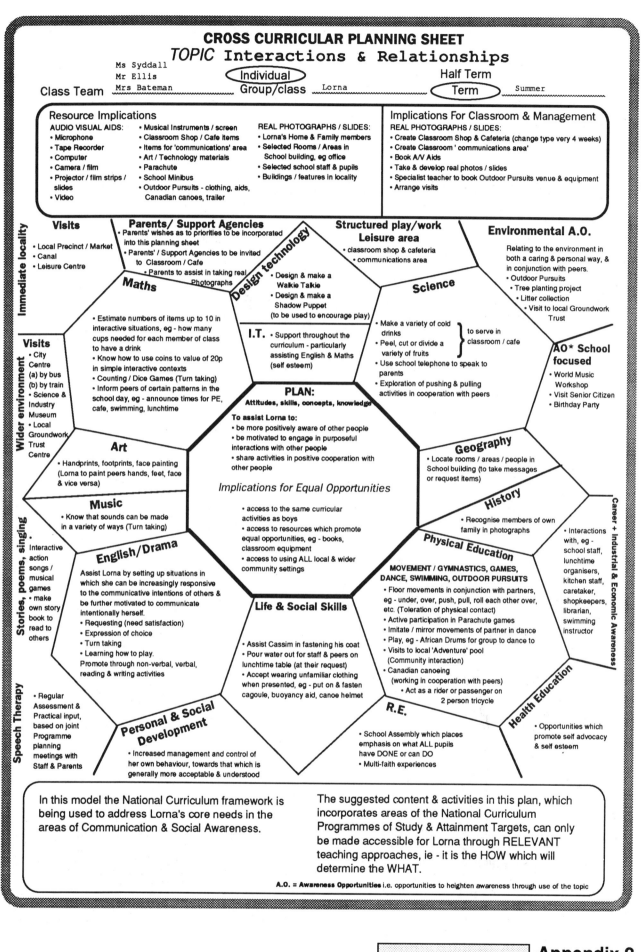

Resource Implications
AUDIO VISUAL AIDS:
- Microphone
- Tape Recorder
- Computer
- Camera / film
- Projector / film strips / slides
- Video

- Musical Instruments / screen
- Classroom Shop / Cafe items
- Items for 'communications' area
- Art / Technology materials
- Parachute
- School Minibus
- Outdoor Pursuits - clothing, aids, Canadian canoes, trailer

REAL PHOTOGRAPHS / SLIDES:
- Lorna's Home & Family members
- Selected Rooms / Areas in School building, eg office
- Selected school staff & pupils
- Buildings / features in locality

Implications For Classroom & Management
REAL PHOTOGRAPHS / SLIDES:
- Create Classroom Shop & Cafeteria (change type very 4 weeks)
- Create Classroom ' communications area'
- Book A/V Aids
- Take & develop real photos / slides
- Specialist teacher to book Outdoor Pursuits venue & equipment
- Arrange visits

Immediate locality

Visits
- Local Precinct / Market
- Canal
- Leisure Centre

Parents/ Support Agencies
- Parents' wishes as to priorities to be incorporated into this planning sheet
- Parents' / Support Agencies to be invited to Classroom / Cafe
- Parents to assist in taking real Photographs

Structured play/work Leisure area
- classroom shop & cafeteria
- communications area

Environmental A.O.
Relating to the environment in both a caring & personal way, & in conjunction with peers.
- Outdoor Pursuits
- Tree planting project
- Litter collection
- Visit to local Groundwork Trust

Design technology
- Design & make a Walkie Talkie
- Design & make a Shadow Puppet (to be used to encourage play)

Maths
- Estimate numbers of items up to 10 in interactive situations, eg - how many cups needed for each member of class to have a drink
- Know how to use coins to value of 20p in simple interactive contexts
- Counting / Dice Games (Turn taking)
- Inform peers of certain patterns in the school day, eg - announce times for PE, cafe, swimming, lunchtime

I.T.
- Support throughout the curriculum - particularly assisting English & Maths (self esteem)

Science
- Make a variety of cold drinks
- Peel, cut or divide a variety of fruits } to serve in classroom / cafe
- Use school telephone to speak to parents
- Exploration of pushing & pulling activities in cooperation with peers

AO* School focused
- World Music Workshop
- Visit Senior Citizen
- Birthday Party

Wider environment

Visits
- City Centre (a) by bus (b) by train
- Science & Industry Museum
- Local Groundwork Trust Centre

PLAN:
Attitudes, skills, concepts, knowledge

To assist Lorna to:
- be more positively aware of other people
- be motivated to engage in purposeful interactions with other people
- share activities in positive cooperation with other people

Implications for Equal Opportunities
- access to the same curricular activities as boys
- access to resources which promote equal opportunities, eg - books, classroom equipment
- access to using ALL local & wider community settings

Art
- Handprints, footprints, face painting (Lorna to paint peers hands, feet, face & vice versa)

Geography
- Locate rooms / areas / people in School building (to take messages or request items)

History
- Recognise members of own family in photographs

Stories, poems, singing
- Interactive action songs / musical games
- make own story book to read to others

Music
- Know that sounds can be made in a variety of ways (Turn taking)

English/Drama
Assist Lorna by setting up situations in which she can be increasingly responsive to the communicative intentions of others & be further motivated to communicate intentionally herself.
- Requesting (need satisfaction)
- Expression of choice
- Turn taking
- Learning how to play.
Promote through non-verbal, verbal, reading & writing activities

Physical Education
MOVEMENT / GYMNASTICS, GAMES, DANCE, SWIMMING, OUTDOOR PURSUITS
- Floor movements in conjunction with partners, eg - under, over, push, pull, roll each other over, etc. (Toleration of physical contact)
- Active participation in Parachute games
- Imitate / mirror movements of partner in dance
- Play, eg - African Drums for group to dance to
- Visits to local 'Adventure' pool (Community interaction)
- Canadian canoeing (working in cooperation with peers)
- Act as a rider or passenger on 2 person tricycle

Career + Industrial & Economic Awareness
- Interactions with, eg - school staff, lunchtime organisers, kitchen staff, caretaker, shopkeepers, librarian, swimming instructor

Life & Social Skills
- Assist Cassim in fastening his coat
- Pour water out for staff & peers on lunchtime table (at their request)
- Accept wearing unfamiliar clothing when presented, eg - put on & fasten cagoule, buoyancy aid, canoe helmet

R.E.
- School Assembly which places emphasis on what ALL pupils have DONE or can DO
- Multi-faith experiences

Health Education
- Opportunities which promote self advocacy & self esteem

Speech Therapy
- Regular Assessment & Practical input, based on joint Programme planning meetings with Staff & Parents

Personal & Social Development
- Increased management and control of her own behaviour, towards that which is generally more acceptable & understood

---

In this model the National Curriculum framework is being used to address Lorna's core needs in the areas of Communication & Social Awareness.

The suggested content & activities in this plan, which incorporates areas of the National Curriculum Programmes of Study & Attainment Targets, can only be made accessible for Lorna through RELEVANT teaching approaches, ie - it is the HOW which will determine the WHAT.

A.O. = Awareness Opportunities i.e. opportunities to heighten awareness through use of the topic

Appendix 2
(Fagg, Aherne, Skelton & Thornber 1990)

Bibliography

Aherne,P. (1990) *Working with Parents in the Process of Developing a Communication Curriculum for Preverbal Learners.* Unpublished Study. Manchester University/Polytechnic

Aherne,P. (1990) Citizenship for Joe. In *Cross-Curricular Theme: Citizenship.* Manchester Education Committee

Aherne,P. and Thornber,A. in association with Fagg,S. and Skelton,S. (1990) *Mathematics For All.* David Fulton. London.

Banes, D. (1989) *Developing Interaction in Early Mathematics skills.* Unpublished notes from a course run at Rainbow School, Bedford.

Bates, E., Benigni, L., Bretherton, I., Camaioni, L and Volterra, V. (1977) 'From Gestures to the First Words: On Cognitive and Social Prerequisites' in M. Lewis and L.A. Rosenblum (eds), *Interaction, Conversation and the Development of Language.* Wiley. New York

Bruner, J. (1972) *The Relevance of Education.* Allen and Unwin. London.

Bruner, J. S. (1975) 'The Ontogenesis of Speech Acts'. *Journal of Child Language,* 2, 1-19.

Coupe,J., Barton,L., Barber,M., Collins, L., Levy, D.and Murphy,D. (1985) *The Affective Communication Assessment.* Manchester Education Committee: Melland School

Coupe, J and Golbart, J., (eds) (1987) *Communication Before Speech.* Croom Helm. London.

Coupe, J. and Levy, D. (1985) *The Object Related Schema Assessment Procedure. Mental Handicap.* 13. 22-24.

Crawley, B. (1988) The Growing Voice: *A Survey of Self Advocacy in Adult Training Centres in Great Britain.* London, Campaign for People with Mental Handicap.

Donaldson, M. (1978) *Children's Minds.* Fontana. London.

Fagg, S., Aherne, P., Skelton, S. and Thornber, A. (1990) *Entitlement For All in Practice.* David Fulton. London.

Fagg, S. and Skelton, S. in association with Aherne, P. and Thornber, A. (1990) *Science For All .* David Fulton. London.

Golbart, J. (1988a) Re-examining the Development of Early Communication. In Coupe, J and Golbart, J., (eds) (1987) *Communication Before Speech.* Croom Helm. London.

Goldbart, J. (1988b) Communication for a Purpose. In Coupe, J and Golbart, J., (eds) (1987) *Communication Before Speech.* Croom Helm. London.

Halliday, M. A. K. (1973) *Explorations in the Function of Language.* Arnold. London

Harding, C. G. (1983) Setting the stage for language acquisition: Communication development in the first year. In R. Golinkoff (ed) *The Transition from Prelinguistic to Linguistic Communication.* Laurence Erlbaum. Hillsdale New Jersey.

Kiernan, C. and Reid, B. (1987) *The Preverbal Communication Schedule (PVCS).* N.F.E.R./Nelson. Windsor.

Kiernan, C., Reid, B. and Goldbart, J. (1987) *Foundations of Communication and Language.* Manchester University Press. Manchester.

McConkey, R. (1987) Interaction: The Name of the Game. In B. Smith (ed) *Interactive Approaches to the Education of Children with Severe Learning Difficulties.* Westhill College. Birmingham.

McLean, J and Snyder-McLean, L., (1985) *Developmentally early communicative behaviours among severely retarded adolescents*, Seminal Topic Outline, Hester Adrian Research Centre. University of Manchester.

Mittler, P. (1988) Foreward In Coupe, J and Golbart, J., (eds) (1987) *Communication Before Speech,* Croom Helm. London.

National Curriculum Council (1989) English in the National Curriculum (Key Stage 1) HMSO. London.

National Curriculum Council (1990) *Curriculum Guidance 3. The Whole Curriculum.* NCC. York.

Piaget, J. (1953) *The Origins of Intelligence in the Child.* Routledge and Kegan Paul. London.

Rogers-Warren, A.K., Warren, S.F. and Baer, D.M. (1983) Interactional Basis of Language Learning In K.T. Kernan, M.J. Begab and R.B. Egerton (eds), *Environments and Behaviour: The Adaptation of Mentally Handicapped Persons,* University Park Press. Baltimore.

Schaffer, H. R. (1986) Child Psychology: The Future. *Journal of Child Psychology and Psychiatry,* 27, 761-779.

Uzgiris, I.C. and Hunt, J. McV. (1975) *Assessment in Infancy : Ordinal Scales of Psychological Development.* University of Illinois Press. Urbana, Illinois.

Vygotsky, L. (1978) Mind and Society: *The Development of Higher Psychologocal Processes.* Harvard University Press. Cambridge. Mass.

Webster, A. and Wood, D. (1989) *Children with Hearing Difficulties.* Cassell. London.

Wood, D., Wood, H., Griffiths, A., and Howarth, I. (1986) *Teaching and Talking with Deaf Children.* Wiley. Chichester.